Barker's Delight

Barker's Delight

or, The Art of Angling

Wherein are discovered many rare Secrets very necessary to be known by all that delight in that Recreation, both for catching the Fish, and dressing thereof.

The Second Edition much enlarged.

**By THOMAS BARKER,
an antient practitioner in the said Art**

Eccles. 3.1.11.
There is a time and season to euery purpose under Heauen:
Euery thing is beautifull in his time.

LONDON,
Printed for *Humphrey Moseley,*
and are to be sold at the *Princes Armes*
in St. *Paul's* Church-yard, 1659.

WAKING LION PRESS

The views expressed in this book are the responsibility of the author and do not necessarily represent the position of The Editorium. The reader alone is responsible for the use of any ideas or information provided by this book.

ISBN 1-60096-459-1

Published by Waking Lion Press, an imprint of The Editorium

Additions to original text © 2006 by The Editorium. All rights reserved. Printed in the United States of America.

Waking Lion Press™, the Waking Lion Press logo, and The Editorium™ are trademarks of The Editorium, LLC

The Editorium, LLC
West Valley City, UT 84128-3917
wakinglionpress.com
wakinglion@editorium.com

Dedication

To the
Right Honorable
EDVVARD LORD MONTAGUE,
Generall of the Navy, and one of
The Lords Commissioners
of the Treasury.

Noble Lord,

    I do present this my book as I have named it *Barker's delight*, to your Honour. I pray God send you safe home to your good Lady and sweet Babes. *Amen, Amen.* If you shall find any thing delightfull in the reading of it, I shall heartily rejoyce, for I know you are one who takes delight in that pleasure, and have good judgement and experience, as many noble persons & Gentlem. of true piety & honour do & have. The favour that I have found from you, and a great many more that did and do love that pleasure, shall never be bury'd in oblivion by me. I am now grown old, and am willing to enlarge my little book. I have written no more but my own experience and practise, and have set forth the true ground of Angling, which I have been gathering these threescore yeares, having spent many pounds in the gaining of it, as is well known in the place where I was born and educated, which is *Bracemeale* in the Liberty of *Salop*, being a Freeman and Burgesse of the same City. If any noble or gentle Angler, of what degree soever he be, have a mind to discourse of any of these wayes & experiments, I live in *Henry* the 7th's Gifts, the next doore to the Gatehouse in *Westm.* my name is *Barker*, where I shall be ready, as long as please God, to satisfie them, and maintain my art, during life, which is not like to be long; that the younger fry may have my experiments at a smaller charge than I had them, for, it would be too heavy for every one that loveth that exercise to be at that charge as I was at first in my youth, the losse of my time, with great expenses. Therefore I took it in consideration, and thought fit to let it be understood, & to take pains to set forth the true grounds and wayes that I have found by experience both for fitting of the rods and tackles both for ground-baits and flyes, with directions for the making thereof, with observations for times and seasons, for the ground-baits and flyes, both for day and night, with the dressing, wherein I take as much delight as in the the taking of them, and to shew how I can perform it, to furnish any Lords table, onely with trouts, as it is furnished with flesh, for 16 or 20 dishes. And I have a desire to preserve their health (with help of God) to go dry in their boots and shooes in angling, for age taketh the pleasure from me. My Lord, I am

      Your Honours most humble Servant,
            Thomas Barker.

In praise of M. Barkers excelent Book of Angling.

    Cards, Dice, and Tables pick thy purse;
        Drinking and Drabbing bring a curse.
    Hawking and Hunting spend thy chink;
        Bowling and Shooting end in drink.
    The fighting-Cock, and the Horse-race
        Will sink a good Estate apace.
    Angling doth bodyes exercise.
        And maketh soules holy and wise:
    By blessed thoughts and meditation:
        This, this is Anglers recreation!
    Health, profit, pleasure, mixt together,
        All sport's to this not worth a feather.

                        Nagrom Notpoh
                                 Armiger.

Encomium in Authorem, Thom. Barkerum.

    Dulcis Molpomene nectarea carmina fundæ
    Ut piscatoris laudes. & gaudia cantem.
    Molli perspicio labentia flumina cursu:
    Lubrica dulcisono crepitantia murmure saxa;
    Atque alto specto ludentes stagmine pisces.
    Sprirantem Zephirum, claro tinctumque
        colore

Coelum: mellifluam musam, volueresq;
 sonantes.
Di[c]e mihi quæ suavis vita, aut quæ blanda
 voluptas
Coequare valet piscandi encomia magna?
Ad Lectorem.
Hic liber eximium cursum semitamque
 docebit
Ambrosea timidos escâ deludere pisces,
Vix faucem poterant hami vitare dolosi:
Artem piscandi generosam expandit amoene,
Amnigenos pisces & arundine vincere longa.
Hic coquus set expers pisces lixare recaptos,
Atque parare suis socius, Convivia rara.

Edmund Swetenham
Gen. Cestriens.

An Encomium on Mr. Barker's exquisite Book of the Art of Angling, &c.

In Helicon though I could dip my quill,
To erect my muse and fathom out thy skill:
Alas! too cheap for that which cost so dear;
Great pains, expence and time, full threescore
 year.
Thou hast unbowell'd brave Dame Natures
 part

In a Vade mecum, with Heroick art.
Thy Booke's a mirrour, there a perfect view
Will still remain, to speak thy praises due.
Perhaps some Rustick currishly will bark
At thee, brave Barker: but if in the dark
And silent night thou canst the knave espie,
With the captive Trout he soon shall make a die.
Then rogues thy name wil dread, & from thee gallop
As from the Devil, when 'tis but Tom of Salop.
But thou ingenuous spirit, follow him
To christall streames, where nimble fish do swim
With fins display'd, and skipping up the streames:
Then (without help of Phoebus glorious beams)
The Trout shall gorge thy bait with pleasure store;
Sweet Philomel shall eccho on the shore.
What now remains? thou hast ensnar'd the fish,
And *Barkers Art* will make a princely dish.

Edward Hopton
Gen. Hamtoniensis.

Friendly Verses in commendation of Mr. Barker's complete work of the Art of Angling.

   Organa piscatorum, ac esca, frequentia piscis,
   Tempora piscandi prima, Culina sciens:
   Omnia *Barkeri* præbet liber aureus ista.
   Artis præceptor cedito, disce, tace.
   Discipulos docuit transfigere, ludere lymphæ,
   Exhaurire: Petri demito rete, beas.
     Thus Englished.
  Tackle, Baits, Fish-haunts, skilfull Cookery,
    Best times to fish, these Barker doth descry.
  To strike, play, land thy prize, he tells thee
    how;
    Art angling teachers all to him must bow.
  Keep thee but from S. Peters net, and then
    Blest be thy soul for aye, Amen, Amen.

                          John Perch
                                Armig.

Pleasant Hexameter Verses in praise of Mr. Barkers Book of Angling.

  Trout, Carp, Perch, Pike, Roch, Dace, Eele,
    Tench, Bleke, Gudgeon, Barbell,
      Thy truth, experience, love, care, cost, skill,
      doth describe well.

Valiant, just, honest, true-hearted,
   ShrewsburyBarker,
   The Art of Angling discovereth, hitherto
   darker
Than either Fowling, Hawking, or hunting the
   swift Hare,
   Markam, *Ward*, *Lawson*, dare you with *Barker*
   now compare?
Of Trouts and huge Pikes you teach us to
   catch a good dish;
   How to make tackle, to kill, and cook also
   all fish.
All we good Brethren of the Angle do give
   you your due praise;
   But on old *Tom*'s head we mean to put the
   crown of Baies.

John Hockenhull
Armig. Cestriensis.

On the choyce Treatise called Barker's Delight.

Come come, ye bunglers, learn the skill
The greedy nimble trout to kill.
For twelve pence (now) thou maist learn more
Than in an age was known before;
All baits to know, tackle to fit,

Brave *Barker* I commend thy wit.
What, catch thy Prey, and cook the Fish?
And more than this, Sir, can you wish?

> Radulphus Hoptonus
> *Gen. Wigorniens.*

In Barkeri librum de arte piscandi Encomium.

Barkeri in laudem, lector, latrare nolito,
    Nam mordere queat dentibus absq; suis.
Vincere si pisces cupias, documenta memento
    Aurea, scripta libro commoditate tuâ.

Bark not at Barker, lest he bite;
    But if in angling thou delight,
To kill the Trout, and cook the Fish,
    Follow his rules and have thy wish.

> Per Morganum Hoptonum
> *Armig.*

The Art of Angling

Noble Lord,

Under favour I will complement and put a case to your Honour. I met with a man, and upon our discourse he fell out with me, having a good weapon, but neither stomach nor skil; I say this man may come home by Weeping cross, I will cause the Clerk to toll his knell. It is the very like case to the gentleman Angler that goeth to the River for his pleasure: this Angler hath neither judgement nor experience, he may come home light laden at his leisure.

A man that goeth to the River for his pleasure, must understand when he cometh there to set forth his tackle: The first thing he must do, is to observe the Sun and the Wind for day, the Moon, the Stars, and the wanes of the Aire for night, to set forth his tackles for day or night, and accordingly to go for his pleasure and some profit.

For example. The Sun proves cloudy, then must you set forth either your ground bait tackles, or of the brightest of your flyes. If the Sun prove bright and clear, then must you put on the darkest of your flyes; thus must you to work with your flyes, light for darkness, and dark for lightness, with the wind in the South, which blowes the fly in the Trouts mouth. Though I set down the wind in the South, I am indifferent where the wind standeth, either with ground-bait or menow, so that I can cast my bait into the River. The very same observation is for night as for day; for, if the Moone prove clear, or the Stars glitter in the sky, it is as ill angling that night as if it were high noon in the midst of the summer, when the Sun shineth at the brightest, wherein there is no hopes of pleasure.

I will begin to angle for the Trout, and discourse his qualitie.

The first thing you must gain must be a neat taper rod light before, with a tender hasel top which is very gentle, with a single hair of five lengths long, one tyed to another, for the bottom of my line, and a line of three haired links for the uppermost part, and so you may kill the greatest Trout that swims, with sea-room.

Now I say he that angles with a line made of three haired links for the bottom, and more at the top, may kill fish, but he that angles with a line made of one haired link, shall kill five to the others one; for, the Trout is very quick-sighted, therefore the best way either for night or day is to keep out of sight.

You must angle alwayes with the point of the rod down the stream, for trouts have not quickness of sight so perfect up the stream as they have opposite against them.

But observe the seasonable times. For example, we begin to angle in *March*: if it prove cloudy, you may angle with the ground baits all day long: but if it prove bright and clear, you must take evening and morning, or else you are not like to do good: so times must be observed and truly understood; for when an angler cometh to the River for his pleasure, and doth not understand to set forth his tackles fit for the time, it is as good keep them in the bag as to set them forth.

Now I am determined to angle with the ground baits, and set my tackles to my rod, and go to my pleasure. I begin at the uppermost part of the stream, carrying my line with an upright hand, feeling my plummet running truly on the ground some ten inches from the hook, plumming my line according to the swiftness of the stream I angle in, for one plummet will not serve for all streams; for the true angling is that the plummet run truly on the ground.

For the bait, the red knotted worm is very good, where Brandlins are not to be had; but Brandlins are better.

Now I will shew you how to make these Brandlins fit to angle with, and to make them lusty and fat, that they may live long on the hook, which causeth the best sport; for that is a chief point, and causeth the best sport.

You must take the yolk of an egg, and some eight or ten spoonfulls of the top of new milk, beaten well together in a porringer, warm it a little until you see it curdle, then take it off the fire and set it to cool; when it is cold, take a spoonful and drop it on the moss in an earthen pot, every drop about the bigness of a green pease, shifting your moss twice in the summer, and once a week in the winter. Thus doing, you shall feed your worms and make them fat and lusty, that they will live long and be lusty and lively on your hook. And thus you may keep them all the year long. This is my true experiment for the ground baits, with the running line for the trout.

My Lord, I will now shew the angling with a Menow (called in some places Pincks) for the Trout, which is a pleasant sport, and killeth the greatest fish: The Trout cometh boldly at the bait, as if it were a Mastiffe dog at a Beare; you may angle with greater Tackles and stronger, and be no prejudice in your Angling. A line made of three silks and three hairs twisted for the uppermost part of your line, and a line made of two silks and two hairs twisted for the bottom next your hook, with a swivel nigh the middle of your line, and an indifferent long hook. But if you can attain to angle with a line of foure haired links for the uppermost part, and a line of three haired links for the bottom, for the finer you angle with, it is the better.

Now I must shew you how to bait the menow on your hook: You must put your hook through the lowermost part of the menow's mouth, so draw your hook through; then put the hook in at the mouth again, let the point of the hook come out at the hindmost fin; then draw your line and the menow's mouth will close, that no water get into its belly; you must be alwayes angling with the point of your rod down the stream, drawing your menow up the side of the stream by little & little, nigh the top of the water; the trout seeing the bait, cometh at it most fiercely; give a little time before you strike. This is the true way without lead, for many times I have had them come at the lead and forsake the menow. He that trieth shall prove it in time.

My Lord, I will shew you the way to angle with a flye, which is a delightfull sport.

The rod must be light and tender, if you can fit your self with a hasel of one piece, or of two pieces set together in the most convenient manner, light and gentle. Set your line to your rod, for the uppermost part you may use your own discretion, for the lowermost part next your flye it must be of three or four haired links. If you can attain to angle with a line of one hair, two or three links one tyed to another next your hook, you shall have more rises and kill more fish. Be sure you do not overload your self with lengths of your line. Before you begin to angle make a triall, having the wind on your back, to see at what length you can cast your flye, that the flye light first into the water, and no longer, for if any of the line fall into the water before the flye, it is better uncast than thrown. Be sure you be casting alwayes down the stream with the wind behind you, and the Sun before you. It is a speciall point to have the Sun and moon before you, for the very motion of the rod drives all the pleasure from you, either by day or by night in all your anglings, both with worms and flyes, there must be a great care of that.

Let us begin to angle in March with the flye. If the weather prove windy or cloudy, there are severall kinds of Palmers that are good for that time.

First, a black Palmer ribbed with silver. Secondly, a black Palmer ribbed with an orenge-tawny body. Thirdly, a black Palmer made all of black. Fourthly, a red Palmer ribbed with gold. Fifthly, a red palmer mixed with an orenge tawny body of cruell. All these flyes must be made with hackles, and they will serve all the year long morning and evening, windy or cloudy. Without these flyes you cannot make a dayes angling good. I have heard say that there is for every moneth in the year a flye for that moneth; but that is but talk, for there is but one monethly flye in the yeare, that is the May-flye. Then if the aire prove clear you must imitate the Hawthorn flye, which is all black and very small, the smaller the better. In May take the May flye, imitate that. Some make it with a shammy body, and ribbed with a black hair. Another way it is made with sandy hogs hair ribbed with black silk, and winged with Mallards feathers, according to the fancy of the angler, if he hath judgement. For first, when it comes out of the shell, the flye is somewhat whiter, then afterwards it growes browner, so there is judgement in that. There is another fly called the oak-flye that is a very good flye, which is made of orenge colour cruell and black, with a brown wing, imitate that. There is another flye made with the strain of a Peacocks feather, imitating the Flesh-flye, which is very good in a bright day. The Grasse-hopper which is green, imitate that. The smaller these flyes be made, and of indifferent small hooks, they are the better. These sorts which I have set down will serve all the year long, observing the times and seasons, if the angler have any judgement. Note the lightest of your flies for cloudy and dark, and the darkest of your flyes for the brightest dayes, and the rest for indifferent times; a mans own j[u]dgement with some experience must guide him: If he mean to kill fish he must alter his flyes according to these directions. Now of late I have found that hogs wooll of several colours makes good bodies, & the wooll of a red heifer makes a good body, and beares wooll makes a good body: there are many good furres that make good bodies: and now I work much of hogs wooll, for I finde it floateth best and procureth the best sport.

The naturall flye is sure angling, and will kill great store of trouts with much pleasure. As for the May flie you shall have him playing alwayes at the rivers side, especially against rain: the Oak flie is to be had on the but of an oak or an ash, from the beginning of May to the end of August; it is a brownish flie, and standeth alwaies with his head towards the root of the tree, very easie to be found: the small black fly is to be had on every hathorn tree after the buds be come forth: your grasse-hopper which is to be had in any medow of grass in June or July. With these flies you must angle with such a rod as you angle with the ground bait: the line must not be so long as the rod, drawing your flye as you find convenient in your angling! When you come to the deep waters that stand somewhat still, make your line two yards long or thereabouts, and dop or drop your flye behind a bush, which angling I have had good sport at; we call it *dopping*.

My Lord sent to me at Sun going down to provide him a good dish of Trouts against the next morning by sixe of the clock, I went to the door to see how the wanes of the aire were like to prove. I returned answer, that I doubted not, God willing, but to be provided at his time appointed. I went presently to the river, and it proved very dark, I drew out a line of three silks and three hairs twisted for the uppermost part, and a line of two hairs and two silks twisted for the lower part, with a good large hook: I baited my hook with two lob-worms, the four ends hanging as meet as I could guess them in the dark, I fell to angle. It proved very dark, so that I had good sport angling with the lob worms as I do with the flye on the top of the water; you shall hear the fish rise at the top of the water, then you must loose a slack line down to the bottom as nigh as you can guess, then hold your line strait, feeling the fish bite, give time, there is no doubt of losing fish, for there is not one among twenty but doth gorge the bait; the least stroke you can strike fastens the hook and makes the fish sure; letting the fish take a turn or two you may take the fish up with your hands. The night began to alter and grow somewhat lighter, I took off the lob-worms and set to my rod a white Palmer-flye, made of a large hook;

I had sport for the time untill it grew lighter; so I took off the white Palmer and set to a red Palmer made of a large hook; I had good sport untill it grew very light: then I took off the red Palmer and set to a black Palmer; I had good sport, made up the dish of fish. So I put up my tackles and was with my Lord at his time appointed for the service.

These three flyes with the help of the lob-worms serve to angle all the year for the night, observing the times as I have shewed you in this night-work, the white flye for darknesse, the red flye in *medio*, and the black flye for lightnesse. This is the true experience for angling in the night, which is the surest angling of all, and killeth the greatest Trouts. Your lines may be strong, but must not be longer then your rod.

> The rod light and taper, thy tackle fine,
>   Thy lead ten inches upon the line;
> Bigger or lesse, according to the stream,
>   Angle in the dark, when others dream:
> Or in a cloudy day with a lively worm,
>   The Brandlin is best, but give him a turn
> Before thou do land a large wel grown Trout.
>   And if with a flye thou wilt have about,
> Overload not with links, that the flye nay fall
>   First on the stream, for that's all in all.

The line shorter than the rods, with a naturall flye:
But the chief point of all is the cookery.

Now having taken a good dish of Trouts I presented them to my Lord. He having provided good company, commanded me to turn Cook and dress them for dinner. Whereu[pon] I gave my Lord this bill of fare, which did furnish his table as it was furnished with flesh.
Trouts in broth, which is restorative, which must be boyled in milk, putting to it some large mace, letting it boyle up. Before you put the trouts into the Kettle, the trouts must be drawn and clean washed before you put them in. So keep them with high boyling, untill you think them boyled sufficient. Then you must take a slice or two of good sweet butter and put into your dish, so pour on the broth, having provided the yolks of half a dozen eggs, being very well beaten in a dish or porringer, pour it into your broth, so stir it well; I make no doubt it will be good broth.

The broth eaten, provide for the sauce some butter, the inner part of a lemmon, the yolk of an egge well beaten together, so pour it into the dish, I make no doubt but it will be well liked of. If they doe not like of this broth, when you boyle other trouts for the service, let the trouts be boyled sufficiently in such liquor as I will shew you now following. You may take the quantity of a quart of the top of the liquor with half a pint of Sack, boyle it together, then provide the yolks of halfe a dozen eggs well beaten together; beat all this together with a slice or two of good sweet butter; no doubt but this will be very good.

Now we must have two dishes of calvored Trouts hot. For the first course the sauce shall be butter and vinegar, 2 or 3 Anchoves, the bones taken out, beaten together with the yolk of one egge for one of the dishes, with a lemmon squeezed on them. For the other dish the sauce and purtenances shall be a quart of oysters stewed in half a pint of Whitewine, so put on the fish, then butter and vinegar being well beaten, with the yolk of an egge poured on that, squeezing a lemmon on the fish, there is no doubt but they will be eaten with delight.

Out of this kettle we must have two dishes to eat cold for the latter course.

First I will shew you the punctuall boyling and calvoring of four dishes.

You must draw out the entrails of the fish, cutting the fish two or three times crosse the backe, lay them on a tray or platter, sprinkle a little salt on them, you must have a quart of vinegar put in a skellet and let it boyle, when it boyles take it off the fire and pour it upon your fish, you shall see your fish rise presently, if they be new, and there is no doubt of calvoring; you must put so much water in your kettle as you think will cover them; you must put in a handful of salt, some rosemary, thyme, and sweet marjoram in a bunch; then you must make this liquor boyle with a fierce fire made of wood: when the liquor hath boyled very well, put in your fish by and by untill you have put in all, keeping them boyling, having provided a cover for your kettle, so put on the cover; you must have a pair of bellows to blow up your fire with speed, that the liquor may boyl up to the top of the kettle, then put in the vinegar that you poured on them before you put them into the kettle, then blow up your liquor with a fierce fire, for the fierce boyling makes the fish to calvor: if the fish be new killed you may let them boyle a quarter of an hour; when they are cold you may put them into a tray or earthen pan, and make such use of them as you have for the the other services, and the rest you may put into a pan untill you have oocasion to use them; be sure they lie covered in the liquor they were boyled in. First put in the one Trout: let one blow up the fire untill the liquor boyle, then put in another; so do untill all are in and boyled.

We must have one dish of Broyled Trouts, when the intrails be taken out, you must cut them across the side: being washed clean, you must take some sweet herbs, as thyme, sweet marjoram, and parlsey chopped very small, the trouts being cut somewhat thick, and fill the cuts full with the chopt herbs, then make your gridiron fit to put them on, being well cooked with rough suet, then lay the Trouts on a charcoal-fire: as you turn them bast them with fresh butter untill you think they are well broyled: the sauce must be butter and vinegar, the yolk of an egge beaten, beat all together and put it on the fish for the service.

To fry a dish of Trouts you must take such a quantity of suet as you shall think sufficient to fry them, and put it in your pan, and be sure that it boyle before you put in your fish, being cut on the side and floured, you must keep them with sitting all the time you are frying them: being fryed sufficiently, when you have dished them the sauce must be butter, vinegar, and some lemmon, but very small, and beaten with your butter and vinegar, then poured on your fish for the service.

The best dish of stewed fish that ever I heard commended of the English, was dressed this way: First they were broiled on a charcoale fire, being cut on the side as fried Trouts, then the stew pan was taken and set on a chaffingdish of coles, there was put into the stew-pan half a pound of sweet butter, one peniworth of beaten cinnamon, a little vinegar; when all was melted the fish was put into the pan, and covered with a covering plate, so kept stewing half an hour, being turned, then taken out of the stew-pan and dished, be sure to beat your sauce before you put it on your fish, then squeeze a lemmon on your fish: it was the best dish of fish that ever I heard commended by Noblemen and Gentlemen. This is our English fashion.

There are divers wayes of stewing; this which I set down last was the English way: But note this, that your stewed trouts must be cut on the side: you may make a dish of stwewed trouts out of your boyling kettle, stewing of them with the same materialls as I did the broiled trouts, I dare warrant them good meat, and to be very well liked.

The Italian he stews upon a chaffing-dish of coles, with whitewine, cloves and mace, nutmegs sliced, a little ginger; you must understand when this fish is stewed, the same liquor that the fish is stewed in must be beaten with some sweet butter and juice of a lemmon, before it is dished for the service. The French doth adde to this a slice or two of bacon, Though I have been no [t]raveller I may speak it, for I have been admitted into the most Ambassadors Kitchins that have come into England this forty years, and do wait on them stil at the Lord Protector's charge, and am paid duly for it: for sometimes I see slovenly scullions abuse good fish most grosly.

We must have a Trout pie to eat hot, and another to eat cold: the first thing you must gain must be a peck of the best wheaten flower, two pound of butter, two quarts of milk new from the Cow, half a dozen of eggs to make the past. Where I was born there is not a girle of ten yeares of age, but can make a pie.

For one pie, the trouts shall be opened, and the guts taken out and clean washed, seasoned with pepper and salt, then laid in the pie, half a pound of currans put among the fish with a pound of sweet butter cut in pieces, and set on the fish, so close it up; when it is baked and come out of the oven, pour into the pie three or four spoonfulls of claret wine, so dish it and serve to the table. These trouts shall eat moist and close.

For the other pie the trouts shall be broyled a little, it will make the fish rise and eat more crisp: season them with pepper and salt and lay them in the pie: you must put more butter in this pie than the other, for this will keep, and must be filled up with butter when it cometh forth of the oven.

There is one good trout of a good length, some eighteen or twenty inches long, we will have that rosted.

You must take out the intrails of this trout with opening the trout one inch at the upper end of his belly, as nigh the gills as you can; then open the trout within one inch of the vent, so you may take the intailes clean out: then wash the trout very clean, keeping the belly whole: then take half a pound of sweet butter, some thyme, sweet marjoram and parsley chopt very small, mix the butter and herbs together and put them into his belly, with half a dozen of oysters, sew up the two slits wih a needle and thred as well as you can: there are broches made to rost a fish, for want of that broch you must take an ordinary broch and spit the fish on; take four or five small laths full the length of the fish, tie those laths on about the fish with a piece of packthred from one end to the other, make the fish fast on the spit, set the spit to the fire; the first thing you bast the fish with must be a little claret wine, next you must bast with butter, with an anchovas beaten together, then bast with the liquor that falleth from the fish untill the fish is rosted; when the fish is rosted take a warm dish and cut the fish off into that dish; then beat the sauce that came from the fish very well, and pour it on the fish, and serve it up.

I will shew you the way to *marionate* a trout or other fish, that it shall keep a quarter of a year in the heat of summer, which is the Italians rarest dish for fresh fish, and will eat perfect and sweet.

You must take out the intrailes and cut them on the side as you do to fry: being washed clean and dried with a cloth, lay them on a tray or board, sprinkle a little salt on them, flower them as to fry them, so take your frying pan with so much suet as when it is melted the fish may lie up to the mid-sides in the liquor, fry them, and every time you turn them flower again, untill you finde that they are fried sufficiently: when you think the fish is dried, take it out of the pan and lay it upon something that the liquor may drein out of it: when the fish is cold you may rear it on end; you must provide a close vessel to keep this fish and liquor in, that no wind can come in, according to the quantity you make triall of; the liquor must be half claretwine, the other half vinegar, two or three bay leaves, so much saffron as a nut tied in a cloth, with some cloves and large mace, and some nutmegs sliced: boyl all this together very well, when the liquor is cold and the fish cold put the liquor into a close vessell, and put the fish into it, then slice three or four lemmons and lay among your fish, make all close that no wind can come into the vessell. After eight or ten dayes you may begin to eat of this fish; the sauce to eat with this fish must be some of the same liquor with some of the sliced lemmon. You must understand that this fish must have a little time before it will come to his kind.

Restorative broth of Trouts learne to make:
Some fry and some stew, and some also bake.

First broyl and then bake, is a rule of good
  skill,
  And when thou dost fortune a great trout to
  kill,
Then rost him, and baste first with good claret
  wine,
  But the colvor'd boyl'd trout will make thee
  to dine
With dainty contentment, both the hot and the
  cold,
  And the marrienate Trout I dare to be bold
For a quarter of a year wil keep to thy mind,
  If covered close & preserved from wind.
But mark well good brother, what now I doe
  say,
Sauce made of Anchoves is an excellent way,
  With oysters and lemmon, clove, nutmeg
  and mace,
  When the brave spotted trout hath been
  boyled apace
With ma[n]y sweet herbs: for forty years I
  In Ambassadours Kitchins learn'd my
  cookery.
The French and Italian no better can doe,
  Observe well my rules and you'l say so too.

I will now shew you the way to take a *Salmon.*
The first thing you must gain must be a rod of
some ten foot in the stock, that will carry a top of

six foot pretty stiffe and strong, the reason is, because there must be a little wire ring at the upper end of the top for the line to run through, that you may take up and loose the line at your pleasure; you must have your winder within two foot of the bottom to goe on your rod made in this manner, with a spring, that you may put it on as low as you please.

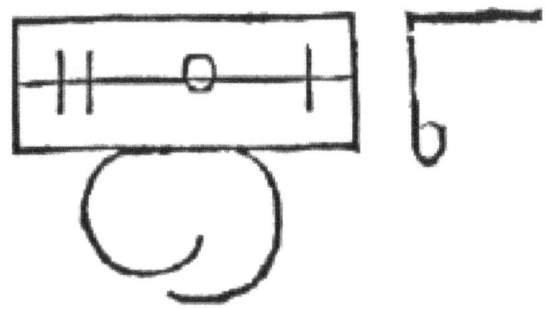

The Salmon swimmeth most commonly in the midst of the river. In all his travells his desire is to see the uppermost part of the river, travelling on his journey in the heat of the day he may take a bush; if the fisherman espy him, he goeth at him with his speare, so shortneth his journey.

The angler that goeth to catch him with a line and hook, must angle for him as nigh the middle of the water as he can with one of these baits: He must take two lob-worms baited as handsomly as he can, that the four ends may hang meet of a length, and so angle as nigh the bo[t]tom as he can, feeling your plummet run on the ground some twelve inches from the hook: if you angle for him with a flie (which he will rise at like a Trout) the flie must be made of a large hook, which hook must carry six wings, or four at least; there is judgement in making those flyes. The Salmon will come at a Gudgeon in the manner of a trouling, and cometh at it bravely, which is fine angling for him and good. You must be sure that you have your line of twenty six yards of length, that you may have your convenient time to turne him, or else you are in danger to lose him: but if you turn him you are very like to have the fish with small tackles: the danger is all in the running out both of Salmon and Trout, you must forecast to turn the fish as you do a wild horse, either upon the right or the left hand, & wind up your line as you finde occasion in the guiding the fish to the shore, having a good large landing hook to take him up.

This fish being killed, if it be not boyled well, then all your labor and pains is lost. If you boyl the fish whole, you must take out the intrailes, cutting the fish three or four times crosse the back, and an inch along the back three or four times crossing the former cuts; by that reason you shall see whether he calvors or no. then you must take a tray according to the length of the Salmon, being dried with a clean cloth; then you must take the Salmon and lay it on the tray, so salt the fish within and without with an indifferent hand, that will give a good relish. Then you must take a quart of the best whitewine vinegar and put it in a skellet and set it on the fire, and let it boyle well and high, so pour it all along on your Salmon, you shall see the Salmon rise presently, and very like to calvor, if the Salmon be new killed, so let it lie untill you are ready to spend it. Then you must take such a pan or kettle that you think the Salmon will lie well in, and set it on the fire made of good drie faggots, and put so much water in the pan or kettle as you think will cover the fish and no more, with two or three handfulls of salt, one pint of vinegar, a good bunch of rosemary, thyme and sweet marjoram tied together, make this liquor boyle very high, then put in your Salmon, having a good paire of bellowes to blow up your fire that the liquor may boyle with speed, then put the vinegar in that was put on the Salmon first, make it boyle up presently, so take your cover and put on, keeping the liquor and Salmon boyling with a fierce fire nigh the space of an hour. If you chine the Salmon and cut the fish in pieces, somewhat lesse boyling will serve. If you keep it to eat cold you must put the liquor and fish all cold together, and make it close, that as little wind come in as you can. If you will eat any of this hot, the sauce is butter, a little vinegar, a lemmon shred very small, beaten together, then the yolks of two eggs beaten & put in the sauce, & beaten very well all together; so being dished pour it on the fish and serve it up to the table, I do not doubt but the dish will be well liked.

> Close to the botom in the midst of the water
> I fished for a Salmon and there I caught her.
> My Plummet twelve inches from the large hook,
> Two lob-wormes hang'd equall, which she never forsook.
> Nor yet the great hook with the six winged flye,
> And she makes at a gudgeon most furiously.
> My strong line was just twenty six yards long,
> I gave him a turne though I found him strong.
> I wound up my tackle to guide him to shore;
> The landing hook helps much, the cookery more.

Now we will see whether we can take a Pike.

There was one of my name the best Trouler for a Pike within this Realm of England: the manner of his trouling was with a hasell rod some twelve foot long, with a ring of wire in the top of the rod for his line to run through: within two foot of the bottom of the rod there was a hole made to put in a winder to turn with a barrell, to gather up his line and loose it at his pleasure. This was his manner of trouling with a small fish.

There are severall other wayes to take Pikes.

There is a way to take a Pike, which is called *the taking a Pike by snap,* for which angling you must have a pretty strong rod, for you must angle with a line no longer than your rod, which must be very strong, that you may hold the fish to it; your hook must be strong and armed with wire of two lengths long: you must bait the fish with the head upwards, and the point must come forth of his side a little above his vent. In all your baitings for a Pike you must enter the needle where the point cometh forth, so draw your arming through untill the hook lieth according as you think fit, them make it fast with a little thred to the wire, so fall to work: the bait must be a Gudgeon if you can get it, or a small Trout, which is the best, or else some other small fish.

Now I will pawn my credit that I will shew a way either in mayre, or pond, or river, that shall take more pikes than any trouler shall do with his rod. And thus it is: First take a forked stick, a line of twelve yards long wound upon it. At the upper end leave a yard either to tie a bunch of fags or a bladder to boy up the fish, to carry the bait from the ground, that the fish may swim clear. The bait must be a live fish, either dace, gudgeon, or roche, or a small trout. The forked stick must have a slit on the one side of the fork, that you may put the line in, that the live fish may swim at that gage you set the fish to swim at, that when the Pike taketh the bait, the Pike may have the full liberty of the line for his feed; you may turne all these loose, either in pond or river all day long, the more the better, and do it in a pond with the wind: at night set a small weight, such as may stay the boy, as a ship lieth at anchor, untill the fish feedeth: for the river you must turn all loose with the stream, two or three be sufficient to shew pleasure. Gaged at such a depth they will goe current down the stream: there is no doubt of pleasure if there be Pikes; the hooks must be double hooks, the shanks must be somewhat shorter than ordinary. My reason is, the shorter the hooks be in the shank, it will hurt the live fish the lesse, and it must be armed with small wire well seasoned: But I hold a hook armed with twisted silk to be better, for it will hurt the live fish the lesse. If you arme your hook with wire, the needle must be made with a hook at the end thereof: if you arm your hook with silk, if it be double the same needle will serve; but if you arm the hook single, the needle must be made with an eye, and then you must take one of the baits alive, which you can get, and with one of your needles enter the fish within a straw breadth of the gill; so put the needle in betwixt the skin & the fish, then put the needle out at the hindmost fin, and so to come forth at the gill, then put on the hook, and it will hurt the live fish the lesse: so knit the arming with the live fish to the line, then put off either in maire or pond, with the wind, in the river, with the stream, the more you put of them in the maire, you are like to have the more pleasure: for the river three or four will be sufficient.

There is a time when pikes go a frogging, and also to sun themselves, there is a speedy way to take them, and not to misse one in twenty. You must take a line made of good twisted thred of some six or eight foot long; arm a large hook of some two inches in the bent betwixt beard and bent, arme it to your line, lead the shank of the hook very handsome, that it may guide the hook at your pleasure; you may strike the Pike where you please, as you see good, with the bare hook. This line and hook doth goe beyond all snaring.

The principall sport to take a Pike is to take a Goose, or Gander, or Duck, take one of the Pikes lines, as I have shewed you before, tie the line under the left wing and over the right wing, as a man weareth his belt, turne the Goose off in a pond where Pikes are, there is no doubt of pleasure betwixt the Goose and the Pike. It is the greatest pleasure that a noble Gentleman in Shropshire giveth his friends for entertainment.

There is no question among all this fishing but we shall take a brace of good Pikes.

I will now shew you the way to dresse them.

The first thing you must doe when the Pike comes in the Kitchin, if it be alive, is to knock the Pike in the head, that the Pike may bleed, then take an handfull of salt and water, so rub him and scoure him to take the slime off, or else there will be durty meat; then take out the intrailes, cut the Pike crosse the back two or three times, salt it well within and without, set on your Kettle with so much water as will cover the Pike, put in three or four handfulls of salt, some good rosemary, thyme, sweet marjoram, tied together, three or 4 onions, so make your liquor boyle very high with a good fire made of dry faggots, then put in your pike, having your bellowes to blow up the fire that the liquor may boyle up to the top of the Kettle for the space of half an hour, by that time it may be boyled sufficiently; then take the Kettle off the fire, then provide a quart of oysters and stew them in half a pint of white-wine; then take half a pound of good butter, you may take a little of the liquor off the top of the Kettle, beat the butter and liquor together with 2 or 3 anchoves, the skin taken off and the bones taken out, with a piece of lemmon chopped very small, beat all these together, beat the yolk of an egge & put it into the sauce, then beat all together, so dish your

Pike, put the oysters on first, then pour on your sauce, there is no doubt but it will be good victualls.

In the Country where I was born we had spits made of iron to rost a Pike or a Carp; you must take water and salt and rub the fish well to take the slime off. To take the intrailes out you must open the fish, cutting the fish an inch in the uppermost part of the belly, and one inch at the vent, so you may take out the intrailes and keep the belly whole: wash the Pike cleane, take halfe a pound of sweet butter, mix the butter with sweet herbs well chopped, put in the Pikes belly with halfe a dozen of oysters, make your cuts as close as you can. For want of such a broch you must have four or five thin laths, so tie the fish on with some packthred from one end to the other, so set your spit to the fire to rost; when it begins to dry a little, take three or four spoonfulls of Claret wine, and baste it first therewith, then take a quarter of a pound of good butter and melt it in a porringer; take two or three anchoves, the skin taken off and bones taken out, beat the butter and anchoves together untill the anchoves be dissolved, then baste the fish with that next, so baste all along with that liquor that falleth from the fish, then warme the dish that must goe to the table, and cut the packthred and let it fall into that dish, so take the liquor that is fallen from the fish and beat it very well together, and pour it on the fish, squeezing a lemon or two on the fish, no doubt but the fish will be eaten and wel liked.

A Rod twelve foot long, and a ring of wire,
A winder and barrell will help thy desire
In killing a Pike, but the forked stick
With a slit and a bladder, and that other fine trick,
Which our Artists call Snap, with a Goose or a Duck,
Will kil two for one if thou have any luck.
The Gentry of Shropshire do merrily smile,
To see a Goose and a belt the fish to beguile.
When a Pike suns himselfe and a frogging doth go,
The two inched hook is better I know
Than the ord'nary snaring: but still I must cry
When the Pike is at home minde the cookery.

To take a Carp either in pond or river, if you mean to have sport with some profit, you must take a peck of ale graines and a good quantity of blood, so mix the the blood and graines together, casting it in the place where you mean to angle; this will gather all the scale-fish together, as Carp, Tench, Roch, Dace, and Bream. The next morning be at your sport very early: plumme your ground, you may angle for the Carp with stronger tackles than ordinary, with a strong line; for your roch and Dace you must angle with fine tackles as single haired lines, if you mean to have sport: the bait must be either a knotted worme or paste for a Carp, but for your Roch and Dace your bait must be either wormes, paste, or gentles, or cadice, or a flye. There is no doubt of sport.

> Late in the evening the ale graines and blood,
> Being well mixt together is bait very good
> For Carp, Tench and Roch, and Dace to prepare,
> If early in the morning at the river you are.
> Strong tackle for Carp; for Roch and Dace fine,
> Will help thee with fish sufficient for to dine.
> For the Carp let thy bait the knotted worm be,
> The rest love the cadice, the paste and the flye.

To take a Perch, The Perch feeds well if you light where they be, and biteth very free. My opinion with some experience is to feed with lob-worms chopped in pieces over night; so in the morning betimes, plumming your ground, gaging your line, bait with a red knotted worm, but I hold a menow to be better to bait: put your hook in at the back of the menow betwixt the flesh & the skin, that the menow may swim up and down, your line being boyed up with a cork or quill, that the menow may swim up and down a foot from the ground, there is no doubt of sport and profit.

For the *Chub* and *Barbell* I have no minde to spend much time, because I do not love them, the reason is, because the fish is very full of bones, and in my opinion they are good no way but baked in a pot, putting into the pot half a pint of Claret to dissolve the bones, and then you may eat them somewhat safely. For the Chub you may angle with a flye or a black snaile; and if you take him, if you do not like that way of dressing, you may slit the fish along the back, the scales being taken off, and the intrails taken out, and flower it, so fry it: see whether this dressing is better than baking. A good sauce may make the fish eat better: the sauce is butter, a little vinegar, with a lemmon chopped very small, beaten well together. This may make the fish eat the better.

For the Barbell, I have taken great ones in *Ware* river with wormes, for I know no better bait than wormes: you have a kind of fishing for them at *London* bridge with three or four hooks fixt to a line with a great plummet, so scratch for them. I was acquainted with *Nicholas Harridans* that lived nigh Algate, who hath killed many a dish of Barbells that way with scratching, and he would tell me that they were good souced & no other way, but I have eaten some boyled, but I did not fancy them.

The *Gudgeon* is a dainty fish to eat being dressed when they are new taken, either fried or boyled, and bites very well. If you come where they are you must angle for them with fine tackle, plummed, that your bait goeth nigh the ground with cork or quill: for the bait, there is a worm which is a little short worme, and is called a Gildtaile, which is the best bait I know for them. For the dressing, you may take your choice, either boyled or fryed; the sauce is butter and a little vinegar, to give the relish, well beaten together, with a little piece of a lemmon to squeeze on them. I make no question but you will like them well.

There are many wayes to take *Eeles:* I will shew you a good way to take a dish of Eeles. When you stay a night or two to angle in a river or pond, take four or five lines of some twelve or fourteen yards long, & every two yards make a noose to hang a hook armed with double thred, for it is better than wire. Bait your hooks with millers thumbs, loaches, menows, or gudgons, tie to every line a hook baited. The lines must be laid cross the river in the deepest places, either with stones or pegged, so that the line lay close to the bottom of the river, there is no doubt of taking a dish of Eeles. You must have a small needle with an eye to bait your hooks.

There is a fish in my Countrey (*viz.* Shropshire) called a *Grayling*, which swimmeth in the gallant river of *Severn*, and all the summer lie in the shallow streams of the River, and cometh very free at the top of the water, with much delight and profit. The manner of angling for him is with a good long rod with casting. The bait must be either a small artificiall or a nature flye. The oak flye is easie to be had there, either on the butt of an oak or the butt of an ash. Sometimes these flyes will not be found, then you must provide some cod bait, they lie in a gravelly husk under stones in most small rivers. The May-flye breedeth on that worm, and doth continue until the end of May. This fish is a dainty eating fish; you may make as many good eating dishes of it as of a Trout, four severall wayes.

Now the way to angle with the Cod bait (as we call it) but named here a cadice, is as followeth.

You must angle with a long rod, but light, your line somewhat longer than the rod. The Grayling feedeth at the top of the water. You must have a little float of cork so big around as a hasell nut, when the fish taketh the bait he flyeth away, so that you shall see the cork flee after the fish, then strike; but you must consider this angling is without lead.

We have Fishermen in that Countrey that will go thirty or forty miles by land, and carry their boat on their back, and so angle down all the way home, with this way of angling, providing a little weele made of wicker to carry their fish, so that they will bring home all their fish alive, whereby they make a very profitable journey.

There comes an honest Gentleman, a familiar freind to me, he was an angler, begins to complement with me and asked me how I did, and when I had been angling, and demanded in discourse, what was the reason I did not relate in my book the dressing of his dish of fish which he loved; I pray you sir, said I, what dish of Trouts was that? He said it was a dish of close boyled Trouts buttered with eggs. My answer was to him, that every scullion dresseth that dish against his will, because he cannot calvor them; I will tell you in short: Put your Trouts into the Kettle when the Kettle is set on the fire, and let them boyle gently, as many Cooks doe, and they shall boyle close enough, which is a good dish buttered with eggs, good for ploughmen, but not for the palate. Sir, I hope I have given you satisfaction.

Now, I will shew you how to make flyes. Learn to make two flyes and make all, that is, the Palmer ribbed with gold or silver, and the Mayflye. These are the ground of all flyes.

We will begin to make the Palmer-flye. You must arm your line on the in-side your hook, then take your sizzers and cut so much of the browne of the Mallards feather as in your owne reason shall make the wings, then lay the outermost part of the feather near the hook, and the point of the feather next toward the shank of the hook, so whip it three or four times about the hook with the same silk you armed the hook with , so make your silk fast; then you must take the hackle of a cock or capon, or a plovers top feather, then take the hackle, silk, or cruell, gold or silver thred, make all fast at the bent of the hook, then begin to work with the cruell, and silver thred, work it up to the wings, every bout shifting your fingers and making a stop, then the cruell and silver will fall right, then make fast, then work up the hackle to the same place, then make the hackle fast; then you must take the hook betwixt your fingers and thumb in the left hand, with a needle or pin part the wings in two, so take the silk you have wrought with all this while, and whip once about the shank that falleth crosse betwixt the wings; than with your thumb you must turn the point of the feather towards the bent of the hook, so view the proportion.

For other flyes, if you make the grounds of hogs wooll, sandy, or black, or white, or the wooll [of] a beare, or of a two-year old red bullock; you must work all the grounds upon a waxed silk, then you must arm and set on the wings, as I have shewed you before.

For the May-flye, you must work with some of these grounds, which it is very good ribbed with a black hair; you may work the body with a cruell, imitating the colour, or with silver suitable to the wings.

For the oak-flie, you must take orenge-colour tawny, and black for the body, and the browne of the Mallards feather for the wings. If you do after my directions they will kill fish, observing the times fitting, and following former directions.

If any worthy or honest Angler cannot hit of these my directions, let him come to me, he shall read and I will work, he shall see all things done according to my foresaid directions. So I conclude for the flye, having shewed you my true experience.

> A Brother of the Angle must alwaies be sped
> With three black Palmers, & also two red,
> And all made with Hackles: in a cloudy day,
> Or in windy weather, angle you may:
> But morning and evening, if the day be bright,
> And the chief point of all is to keep out of
>   sight.
> In the moneth of May, none but the May-flye;
> For every month one, is a pitiful lye:
> The black hawthorn flye must be very small,
> And the sandy hogs haire is sure best of all

For the Mallard wing'd May-flye; and the
    Peacocks train
Will look like the flesh-flye to kill Trout
    amaine.
The oak flye is good, if it have a brown wing,
So is the Grashopper that in July doth sing,
With a green body, make him on a midle siz'd
    hook;
But when you have catcht fish, then play the
    good Cook.
Once more my good brother, Ile speak in thy
    eare,
Hogs, red Cows, & Bears wooll, to float best
    appear,
And so doth your fur, if rightly it fall;
But alwayes remember, make two and make
    all.

I could set down as many wayes to dress Eeles as would furnish a Lords table, but I will relate but one.

Take off the skin whole untill you come within two inches of the taile; beginning at the head take out the intrailes, wash the eele clean, dry it with a cloth, scotch it all along on both the sides; take some pepper and salt, mix them together, rub the Eele very well with the pepper and salt; draw the skin on again whole, tie the skin about the head with a little thred lapped round; it must be broyled on a charcole fire, let your gridiron be hot, rub your gridiron well with rough suet, then the skin will neither break nor burn. The Eele will broyl in his own liquor, and will be a good dish. But, take the skin off and stew the Eele betwixt two dishes upon a chaffindish of coles, with sweet butter, a little vinegar, with some beaten cinnamon, that will be a rare dish.

The boyling of a Carp is the very same way as I have shewed you for the Trout, with the scales on; no better sauce can be made than anchoves sauce: The high boyling is the best for all freshwater fish. I have served seven times seven years to see the experiment.

If you desire to make your sauce black, if your Carp be alive, you must take your knife and thrust it about the middle of his belly, then the Carp will bleed; so take a little vinegar and put it in a saucer, and as the blood falleth in stir it about untill all the blood is run. If the Carp be dead, take the cold blood out of the Carp and beat it with your sauce. This is called *black sauce for a Carp.*

If there be any Gentleman that liveth adjoyning to a river side where Trouts are, I will shew him the way to bring them to feed that he may see them at his pleasure. And to bring store to the place, gather great garden-worms, the quantity of a pint or a quart, chop them in pieces and throw them where you intend to have your pleasure; with feeding often there is no doubt of their coming, they will come as sheep to the pen; you must begin to feed with pieces of worms by hand by one and one, untill you see them feed; then you may feed with liver and lights, so your pleasure will be effected.

I have a willing mind with Gods help to preserve all those that love this recreation, to goe dry in their boots and shooes, to preserve their healths, which one receit is worth much more than this book will cost.

First, they must take a pint of Linseed oyle, with half a pound of mutton suet, six or eight ounces of bees wax, and half a pinniworth of rosin, boyle all this in a pipkin together, so let it coole untill it be milk warm, then take a little hair brush and lay it on your new boots; but its best that this stuff be laid on before the boot-maker makes the boots, then brush them once over after they come from him; as for old boots you must lay it on when your boots be dry.

If you want good Tackles of all sorts, you must go to Mr. *Oliver Fletcher* at the west end of Pauls, at the sign of the three Trouts.

If you would have the best Hooks of all sorts, go to *Charles Kirby,* who lives in shooe lane at Harp alley, in Mill-yard.

If you would have a rod to beare and to sit neatly, you must go to *John Hobs* who liveth at the sign of the George behind the Mews by Charing-crosse.

 A live and small minow is the best bait
  To kill a great Pearch by Anglers deceit,
 A black snaile is the bait for the bonny Chub,
  A Barbell souced is meat very good.
 The greedy Gudgeon doth Love the Gild taile,
  And the twelve yard line doth never faile,
 To kill of good Eees an excellent dish,
  With nooses and baits of the little fish;
 At the but of the oak take you the flye,
  And kill the Grayling immediately.
 But when of all sorts thou hast thy wish,
  Follow Barkers advice to cook the fish.
 Think then of the gatehouse, for neere it lives
  he,
  Who kindly will teach thee to make the flye.
 And if thou live by a river side,
  Believe thou thy friend who often hath
  try'd,
 And brought store of fish, as sheep to the pen;
  But friend, let me tell thee once agen,
 His art to keep thee both warm and dry,
  Deserveth thy love perpetually.
 He names three men to thee, like a good
  friend,
  Make use of them all, and so I end.

Noble Lord,

I have found an experience of late, which you may angle with, and take great store of this kind of fish: first, it is the best bait for a Trout that I have sen in all my time, and will take great store, and not faile, if they be there. Secondly, it is a speciall bait for Dace, or Dare, good for Chub, or Bottlin, or Grayling. The bait is the roe of a Salmon, or Trout, if it be a large Trout, that the spawnes be any thing great. You must angle for the Trout with this bait as you angle with the brandlin, taking a paire of cisers and cut so much as a large Hasel nut, and bait your hook, so fall to your sport, there is no doubt of pleasure. If I had known it it but twenty years agoe I would have gained a hundred pounds onely with that bait. I am bound in duty to divulge it to your Honour, and not to carry it to my grave with me. I do desire that men of quality should have it that delight in that pleasure: The greedy Angler will murmur at me, but for that I care not.

For the angling for the scale-fish they must angle either with cork or quill, plumming their ground, and with feeding with the same bait, taking them asunder that they may spread abrod that the fish may feed and come to your place. there is no doubt of pleasure angling with fine Tackles, as single haire lines at least five or six lengths long, a small hook with t[wo] or three spawns, the bait will hold one week. If you keep it on any longer, you must hang it up to dry a little: When you go to your pleasure again, put the bait in a little water, it will come in again.

Sic vale feliciter.

Thomas Barker.

FINIS.